Compagnie National du Rhône—J. Cellard

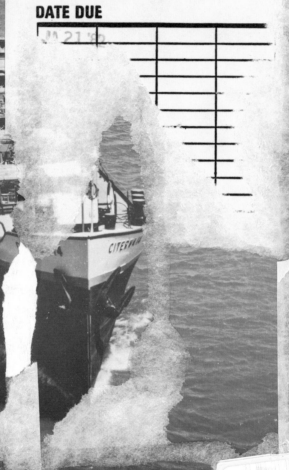

Canal in the lower part

THE Rhone

RIVER OF CONTRASTS

Jean Gabriel Seruzier

Le Pont Saint Bénézet in Avignon.

THE
Rhone
River of Contrasts

by FRANCES WILLARD von MALTITZ

Illustrations by Joanne Isaac
Maps by Fred Kliem

GARRARD PUBLISHING COMPANY
CHAMPAIGN, ILLINOIS

NANCY LARRICK, ED.D.,

IS THE EDUCATIONAL ADVISOR FOR THIS SERIES.

Manufactured in the United States of America
Library of Congress Catalog Number: 65-12535

Swiss National Tourist Office

Contents

How the Rhone Got Its Name 7

1. *Where the Rhone Begins* 9

2. *Valais—The Swiss Valley of the Rhone* . . 21

3. *Lake Geneva* 33

4. *From Switzerland Into France* 38

5. *Lyons, the Crossroads City* 43

6. *Boats on the River* 55

7. *Ancient Ruins and Smoking Factories* . . 59

8. *The Bridge at Avignon* 70

9. *A Castle and a Monster* 77

10. *Through the Delta to the Sea* 80

Index 94

How the Rhone Got Its Name

The Romans called the river Rhodanus. In the course of centuries, the spelling of the word was changed to Rhosne. Finally, as happened in many French words, people put an accent mark over the o, instead of writing s. So the name became Rhône in French.

We don't know what the word Rhodanus means. Some people think that Greek settlers from the island of Rhodes gave their name to the river. According to them, there was an ancient Greek town on the Rhone called Rhodanusia.

But nobody really knows where the word came from. All we can be sure of is that the Rhone is one of the loveliest and most fascinating rivers of Europe.

We can explore its path through the landscape of Europe today. Or we can go back in time and watch history unfold along its banks. It offers adventure to anyone who follows its course.

SEAL OF THE · CITY OF LYONS

THE RHONE VALLEY

STATUTE MILES

0   50   100   150

WEST GERMANY

F R A N C E

LOIRE RIVER

SAÔNE RIVER

DOUBS RIVER

RHINE RIVER

ZURICH

SWITZERLAND

BERN

LAKE GENEVA

GENEVA

RHONE RIVER

SAÔNE RIVER

AIN RIVER

RHONE RIVER

LOIRE RIVER

N

W   E

S

LYONS

ISÈRE RIVER

ITALY

GENOA

DRÔME RIVER

AYGUES RIVER

DURANCE RIVER

RHONE RIVER

DURANCE RIVER

GARD RIVER

MONACO

NICE

MARSEILLES

M E D I T E R R A N E A N   S E A

1. Where the Rhone Begins

Every morning in summer the people in the village of Andermatt, Switzerland, hear the trumpeting notes of a horn. This is the familiar signal of the Alpine buses. When the villagers hear it, they know that the first daily bus has started its climb up the Furka Pass to the Rhone Glacier. From the opposite direction another bus will be coming over the Grimsel Pass from the town of Meiringen. At every hairpin turn of the road, the drivers sound their horns. The cheerful notes warn approaching cars that a big bus is on the other side of the curve.

The great mass of snow on the left is the famous Rhone Glacier.

All along the high roads in the Alps, the sound of these horns can be heard in June. It means that the high passes are free of their winter snow. People can now go up to the awesome land of glaciers and explore the lofty regions of the Alps.

The jagged peaks of these towering mountains seem to touch the sky. Often they disappear in the swirling mists of the clouds. Only daring and experienced climbers can reach the summits.

Somewhat lower down there are automobile

10

From a distance the glacier looks like a tumble of snowy rocks.

roads through the passes. But many of these are closed by snow eight months of the year. Travel in the Alps in winter is made possible by tunnels cut through the great walls of rock. There are tunnels for cars and tunnels for trains, going from one side of a massive range to the other.

The Alps are more than a hundred miles wide in places. They stretch across the borders of Switzerland into Germany, France, Austria and northern Italy.

11

In summer and in winter, snow blankets the highest parts of these mountains. This enormous white mass pushes its way down the slopes. The weight of the snow at the top forces long tongues of ice to inch their way down into the valleys. These slowly moving masses of ice and snow are called glaciers.

There are glaciers of different kinds in many parts of the world. In the Arctic and Antarctic they extend to the sea, where great chunks break off to become floating icebergs. In the Alps the glaciers move slowly down to a lower, warmer level of land. There they gradually melt and run off into mountain lakes and streams.

Glaciers sometimes grow longer, sometimes shorter, depending on the snowfall of the year. But the glacier itself is constantly grinding a path down the mountainside, churning up gravel and clay from the mountain underneath it.

The movement of a glacier is too slow to be seen, but it can be measured by markers in the ice. Like a river, the glacier moves faster in the

12

Roads zigzag toward the Rhone Glacier and into the valley below.

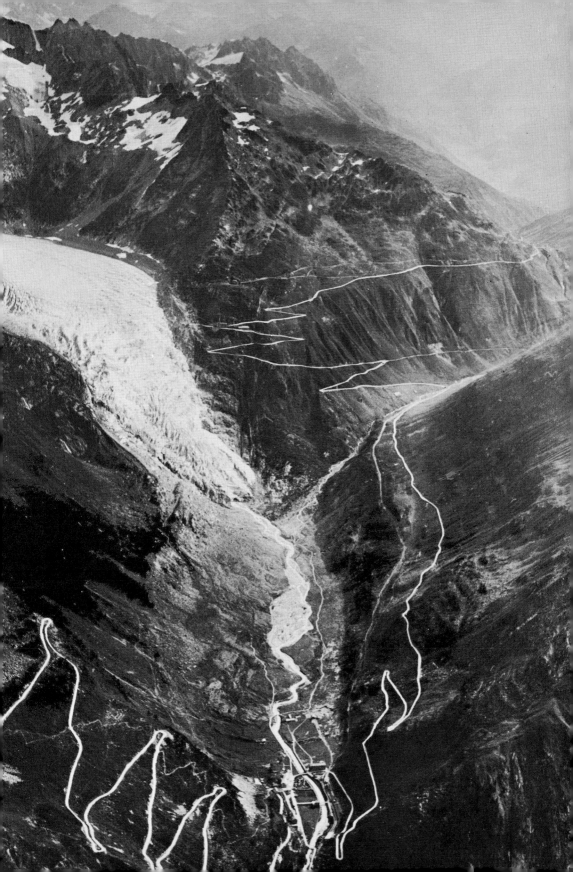

middle than on the edge. Some glaciers move as much as two feet a day.

Even on the highest passes of the Alps, there are inns which have been offering shelter to travelers for more than a hundred years. Some of the earliest shelters were run by monks, like the one on the Saint Bernard Pass. This hostel had big Saint Bernard dogs to help find travelers who were lost in the snow.

When the first inns were built, there were no cars or buses. People came on foot or muleback or in carriages pulled by horses. Sometimes the way was just a narrow track.

Today it takes only a few hours to reach the top of the pass by car. But the mountains have not changed. They are as magnificent as ever.

At a curve of the road on the Furka Pass, the buses stop at an inn called the Belvedere. This means "beautiful view" in Italian. It is a good name, for here the Rhone Glacier comes into sight. It is a greenish mass of ice, streaked here and there with dirt which the glacier has picked

The Furka Pass makes a hairpin turn near the great Rhone Glacier.

up on its path. The glacier ends abruptly as a cracked but massive wall of ice, perched on the edge of a steep drop of rock.

The road curves close to the glacier, so it is possible to get a good look at this wonder of nature. You can walk to the edge of the great frozen river and touch its granular surface. You can go into an ice grotto which has been cut inside the glacier. An eerie greenish light filters through the dripping walls. Sometimes through an

15

Swiss National Tourist Office
High in the Swiss Alps this tiny village is almost buried in snow.

opening in the wall of the grotto, crevices can be seen, splitting the ice down to an unknown depth. Back out in the sunshine, you can see the expanse of ice stretching toward the mountaintops.

There are hundreds of glaciers in the Alps, some of them much larger than the one on the Furka Pass. But this glacier has a very special reason for its fame. At the far side, away from the road but easily seen, a stream comes rushing

16

out and goes tumbling down the rocks toward the valley below. It is the beginning of the Rhone River.

The pitch of the mountain is steep here so the river begins as a series of cascades. The water splashes and sprays and sparkles. Sometimes it splits around a rock, dividing into separate little streams and waterfalls, coming together again farther on.

When it reaches the level floor in the valley below, it passes under its first bridge, a little foot crossing. Here stands another inn called the Hotel of the Glacier *(Hôtel du Glacier)*. It seems too far from the glacier above to be called by its name. But people who know this region will explain that fifty years ago the glacier came all the way down to this point.

Next year the glacier may recede more, or it may begin to grow. But wherever the glacier ends, the Rhone River begins.

At its beginning the Rhone flows past tiny Alpine villages. Here the little dark wooden houses have heavy stones on their roofs to hold them tightly against the earth when storm winds blow.

Big, surefooted cows graze peacefully on the upland meadows. Even before we catch sight of them, moving slowly on the steep hillsides, we can hear their bells. As the animals lift and swing their heads, the music comes softly across the pastures, the jingling and tolling and tinkling of the bells.

The Alpine meadows are dotted with brightly colored wild flowers. There are blue gentian, yellow mountain saxifrage and dark red dwarf primula. If we climb high enough we may even

Spring sunshine converts melting snow into a rushing Alpine stream.
Bachmann for Schweizerische Zentrale für Verkehrsförderung

Gentian   *Anemone*   *Edelweiss*

find a star-shaped velvety white edelweiss ($\bar{a}\acute{y}$-*del-vise*). This is a rare blossom, found usually in high crevices. It has come to be the symbol of the high mountain regions. The French have a very beautiful name for it. They call it "star of the glaciers."

As the Rhone moves on through the valley, it is joined by other streams from the mountain ranges on both sides. In spring and summer the Alps are aglitter with the water coming down their slopes. The mountains seem awash with rivulets, streams and torrents. The sound of running water is everywhere.

Many of the rivers of Europe have their origin in the melting snows of the Alps. There is an old jingle:

> *The Rhone, the Rhine, the Tiber, the Po,*
> *Arise in the Alps, and away they go.*

The shape and slant of the slopes tell which way they will go. The Rhine, for example, begins not far from the Rhone. Its source is only about fifty miles away. The Rhine goes down the north face of the range toward the cold North Sea. The Rhone heads in the opposite direction on its long journey to the sunny Mediterranean.

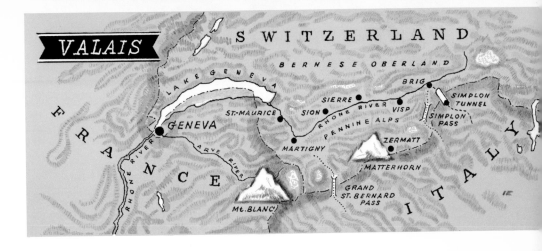

2. Valais – The Swiss Valley of the Rhone

The valley into which the Rhone flows slants toward the southwest. This is the direction of the river for most of its length in Switzerland. The name for this valley is the Valais (*val-eh́*).

It is a steep valley lying between two massive ranges of mountains. To the northwest is a collection of peaks and plateaus called the Bernese Oberland, meaning "the highlands or high country of Bern." On the southeast side of the valley, the Pennine Alps separate Switzerland from Italy.

In the upper part of the Valais, the Rhone passes tiny villages with German names like Münster and Reckingen. Ever since the thirteenth

21

*Farm women
of the Valais
rake their meadows.*
Swiss National
Tourist Office

century this has been a German-speaking section of Switzerland.

These towns along the upper Rhone are clusters of simple wooden houses. They are built on the river's edge or perched dizzily on the steep mountainside. The houses are made of tough larch wood, which weathers to a color almost black. Sometimes one sees a little onion-towered church on the edge of the village. And bridges cross the river here and there.

Because the upper Valais is steeply pitched, the Rhone flows swiftly. The water is milky gray

22

Houses and churches are perched on dizzy slopes.

Swiss National
Tourist Office

from the glacial clay it carries along. The Rhone is a frisky and spirited river from its very beginning. As other streams join it, the river grows so strong that there is often danger of its overflowing. To keep it under control, the Swiss have lined it with stone curbs in many places. Even with these embankments the Rhone sometimes goes on a rampage. One night in the summer of 1963, people in the Valais were awakened by the roaring sound of the river flooding over its banks, washing away bridges and buildings. An underground lake higher up had broken out and swelled the Rhone with its waters.

Twenty-eight miles from its source, the Rhone reaches its first big town. This is Brig (or in French spelling, Brigue), an important junction for travelers today. It was a flourishing trading center even in the Middle Ages. The Romans called it "rich Brig."

Brig lies at the foot of the Simplon Pass, which leads over the Alps to Italy. Before the time of airplanes, the only way to get across a mountain

A village scene on Sunday morning.

Schweizerische Zentrale
für Verkehrsförderung

range was to walk or ride horseback over it. People searched out the passes, where the mountains dipped a little lower and were easier to cross. The towns at the foot of the passes were gathering places for travelers.

Until the time of Napoleon, there was only a rough path through the Simplon Pass. Early in the nineteenth century, Napoleon ordered a road built on this route over the Alps. Then in 1906 a railroad tunnel was completed under the pass. The Simplon Tunnel burrows 12½ miles through rocky mountain walls. Now it is possible to cross the

In the steep slopes near Zermatt, a roof has been built over the railroad to keep snow from burying the tracks and trains.

barrier of the Alps at any time of year and in all kinds of weather. So Brig became an important rail junction, linking Switzerland and Italy.

By the time the Rhone reaches Brig, it has dropped almost 4,000 feet, and it races through the town. But below Brig the valley widens and the course of the river levels off. The Rhone flows through a landscape of vineyards and orchards.

Plums, apricots, pears and grapes are raised in this fertile section.

At the little town of Visp, the Visp River tumbles down its own tiny valley to join the Rhone. Rail and auto roads lead up the valley to Zermatt and the spectacular sight of the great triangular peak of the Matterhorn.

The next important town the Rhone passes has two names: Sierre in French and Siders in German. It marks the end of the German part of the Valais. Below Sierre most of the people in the Valais speak French.

Following the Rhone beyond Sierre, we come to Sion, which is the capital of the Swiss province of Valais. Here two little hills rise from the valley, each one topped by a castle. On summer nights the hilltops are lighted while a pageant of music and voices tells the story of the town.

The Romans knew Sion as Sedunum. They planted grapevines here and made the town a pleasant resort for their weary soldiers. The vineyards of Sion still provide good wine.

As far back as the sixth century, Sion was a kind of capital. After the Romans had become Christians, Sion was the headquarters for a bishop. In 999 the Bishop of Sion became the ruler of the province as well as the head of the church. In those days the church had much more power in politics and government than it has today. It was a bishop who built the Castle of Tourbillon in 1294. Its ruins still stand on one of the two hills of Sion today.

The old stones of the Castle of Tourbillon have seen many events in the city's history. They looked down on Sion when the black plague swept

Entrance to the Castle of Tourbillon.
Chemins de fer fédéraux

Chemins de fer fédéraux

The Cathedral at Sion was built in the thirteenth century.

the city in 1348. They saw the city captured by the Count of Savoy and freed again by patriots of Valais. They saw fighting between one group which wanted the Valais to be part of the German Empire and another which favored the French.

When Napoleon came to power in Europe, he declared Valais independent and named it the Rhodanic Republic, after the old word for the Rhone. Later he made it part of France. After Napoleon's fall, the Valais was free and joined the Swiss Federation, with Sion still its capital.

Twenty miles beyond Sion, the Rhone makes a sharp turn north at Martigny. Its way south and west is blocked by the great bulk of the French Alps. Rising above Martigny to the west are the jagged *Dents du Midi*, the "teeth of the south," and farther away to the southwest, the king of the Alps, Mont Blanc. The river Drance, draining these slopes, joins the Rhone at Martigny.

Like Brig, Martigny stands at the foot of an important Alpine pass. It is the beginning of the road to the Great Saint Bernard Pass to Italy.

From Martigny the Rhone moves through a narrow gorge on its way toward Lake Geneva. At one place the river, the railway and the automobile road squeeze through the same narrow passage. This is Saint-Maurice, which gets its name from a Roman military commander of the third century. The story is that Mauritius and his soldiers had become Christians while the Roman Emperor, Maximian, had not. The Emperor ordered all soldiers to worship him and the Roman gods, but Mauritius and his men refused. As they

At the right of this highway near Sion, you see terraced vineyards.

marched through the narrow gorge, they met troops sent by the Emperor to enforce his order. Mauritius and his soldiers fought valiantly, but every one was killed, we are told, in the rocky gorge which we now call Saint-Maurice.

Beyond Saint-Maurice, the Rhone flows into a broad plain. It is marshy and covered with silt carried down by the river in the course of centuries. At the end of the plain lies Lake Geneva. Like a miniature sea it receives and absorbs the Rhone. For some distance out from the shore, you can see the milky river flowing through the lake. Then the two waters merge, and the Rhone disappears in the blue depths of the lake.

This is the end of the Valais and the first part of the Rhone. The river has traveled 105 miles from the glacier to Lake Geneva. In all this length it is too swift and drops too quickly to be navigable. So it is not as a means of transportation that the Rhone has attracted people to the Valais. It has pointed out the natural way through the valley, up from the lake and down from the glacier.

The Tower of the Witches in Sion.
Swiss National Tourist Office

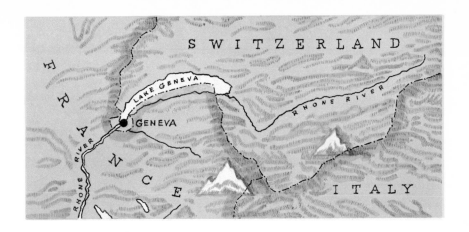

3. Lake Geneva

Lake Geneva, or Lac Léman as the French call it, is crescent shaped and clear blue. The northern side and both ends of the lake are Swiss territory. Its southern shore belongs to France. There are mountains to be seen in all directions, with the French Alps rising sharply from the edge of the water.

At its widest point Lake Geneva is 8½ miles across. Its shores are lined with villas and hotels. The blue expanse of water is dotted with sail-boats, motor launches and steamers, circling and crossing the lake.

The Rhone enters Lake Geneva at its eastern

end. Forty-five miles away to the west, at the other end of the lake, a new Rhone is born.

The lake narrows to end at the city of Geneva. Here a little series of locks or dams control the emerging river. Lord Byron, the English poet, described it as "the blue rushing of the arrowy Rhone." Its color is somewhat muddied now by the wastes of a big city. But its current is swift as an arrow as it comes out of the lake.

The city of Geneva extends along the lakefront and down both sides of the river. Geneva has long been known for the beauty of its surroundings. It has also been famous as an international meeting place. It is the headquarters for the International Red Cross. When the League of Nations was established after World War I, Geneva was chosen as its home. This experiment in international cooperation failed, but Geneva is still a favorite setting for worldwide organizations and conferences.

As early as 1262 trade fairs were held in this city. Merchants came from Italy, Switzerland and

The Rhone flows into Lake Geneva from the Swiss Alps.

France. Like the world fairs of today, these medieval fairs provided an opportunity to see the products and meet the people of other countries. Among the merchandise brought to the fairs at Geneva were silks, armor, wine, timber and salt.

Later there were other reasons for the inter-

Jacques Thévoz for Swiss National Tourist Office

Dams control the river as it pours from the western end of the lake.

national character of Geneva. In the sixteenth century a movement for the reformation of the Catholic church was sweeping Europe. Many of its supporters, called Protestants, were persecuted in their Catholic countries and fled to Geneva. For a long time after this, the city was a refuge for Protestants from Italy, France and England.

A French family which came to Geneva to escape religious persecution at home gave Geneva one of its most famous men—Jean Jacques Rousseau. He was born in Geneva early in the eighteenth century. In this period many brilliant writers and scientists lived in Geneva. But not all of them approved the strange new ideas of Jean Jacques Rousseau. In an age of kings Rousseau thought that people should be governed only with their consent. Men are born good, he said, and are made evil by the bad things in our society. Therefore, he wanted children to be brought up close to nature so they could develop simply and naturally. Today Rousseau is honored as one of the great men of his era. He loved the beauties of nature and wrote much about Lake Geneva and its surroundings. A little island in the lake now bears his name. Just where the Rhone begins to leave Lake Geneva is the tiny Ile Rousseau.

4. From Switzerland Into France

As the Rhone flows from Geneva, its color is greenish blue. Almost immediately it is joined from the left by the river Arve. This river comes down from the snows of Mont Blanc and has the milky look of glacial water. For a time the two streams move side by side in the same channel, each keeping its distinctive color. Then the whitish Arve mixes with the Rhone, turning it greenish gray.

A few miles below Geneva is the first important dam on the Rhone. At Verbois a power plant turns the force of the river into electricity to light the city of Geneva.

Because of the current and the dam, this stretch of the Rhone cannot be used for commerce. But with a good boatman and a dependable motor, one can travel to the dam in a small boat. Going down with the current is easy. Coming back upstream a boatman must hug the shore and choose his course with care. Trees hang over the riverbanks, their boughs trailing in the swirling water.

With so little traffic on the river, flocks of water birds can nest wherever sandbanks form. They rise with a massed fluttering of wings when a little boat passes nearby. Here and there a boy can be seen, fishing from the bank. But mostly

Below the dams, fishermen enjoy the easy current of the river.

the Rhone is undisturbed as it moves on its way toward France.

Just 12 miles from Geneva the Rhone becomes French. On this part of its course, the river flows through narrow ravines. There used to be a place here where the Rhone all but disappeared underground. Now that point has been covered by the lake formed by a great dam.

The Swiss Rhone and the French Rhone are two very different rivers. In Switzerland the Rhone is a lovely part of the mountain landscape. It adds to the beauty of the scene as it frolics down the mountainside. It is a familiar and pleasant companion as it sings its way through the Valais. But it does not play a major part in the economy of the country.

From its very beginning in France, the Rhone is put to work for the French. A few miles inside the French border stands the huge Genissiat Dam. When it was finished in 1948, this was the largest power plant in western Europe. To help control the flow of water from Genissiat, another dam

The huge Genissiat Dam is a few miles inside the French border.

was constructed at Seyssel, 11 miles farther on.

A few miles below the gorges and dams, the Rhone returns to more gentle ways. It flows through a wider valley, past villages which seem untouched by the years. One such tiny village is Vertrieu, a cluster of ancient farmhouses on the bank of the Rhone. On a craggy promontory

41

above the town are the blackened ruins of a medieval castle.

A century or two ago Vertrieu provided rivermen for the boats on this part of the Rhone. No boats could go past the gorges, but there was local traffic on the river. Timber was cut on the hillsides and carried downriver by barge to be made into charcoal. Horses pulled the barges back.

With trucks and trains now providing faster transportation, the river is no longer used commercially around Vertrieu. Today Vertrieu has only 200 inhabitants. A few of its old houses are used as country homes by people from the city of Lyons. The village street looks as it did 200 years ago. But the signs posted for fishermen and campers tell of changes in the Rhone.

Attention! Danger!
It is dangerous to venture into the bed of this river or onto the islands and sandbanks, the water being able to rise abruptly and at any moment as a result of the operations of the hydroelectric plants and dams.

At Lyons the muddy Rhone is joined by the sparkling river Saône.

5. Lyons, the Crossroads City

At Lyons the rushing Rhone is joined by the Saône River, a broad, peaceful stream. The doubled river then goes straight south through France to the sea. All of the Rhone south of Lyons can be used for shipping.

You can travel on the Saône, too, back north to the heart of France. By its joining with the Saône at Lyons, the Rhone becomes part of a great network of canals and rivers connecting the

43

Mediterranean Sea with many parts of France. Boats can go from the Rhone, via the Saône, to the Loire River. They can get to Paris and on to the English Channel, by way of the Seine. It is even possible for small boats to reach the Rhine River from the Rhone through a canal at Mulhouse in northern France. This link makes a connection between the Mediterranean and the North Sea.

Centuries ago Lyons was a tiny settlement. Today it is a sprawling industrial giant extending into the country for miles around. It is the third largest city in France. Only Paris and Marseilles are bigger. Lyons is a busy modern city with textile mills, chemical plants and automobile factories. It also has a long and remarkable past.

Its geographical location has made Lyons a natural crossroads. It stands at the head of a valley leading down to the Mediterranean. From this point where the two rivers meet, you can travel north on the Saône and south on the Rhone. To the east lies a gateway into Switzerland.

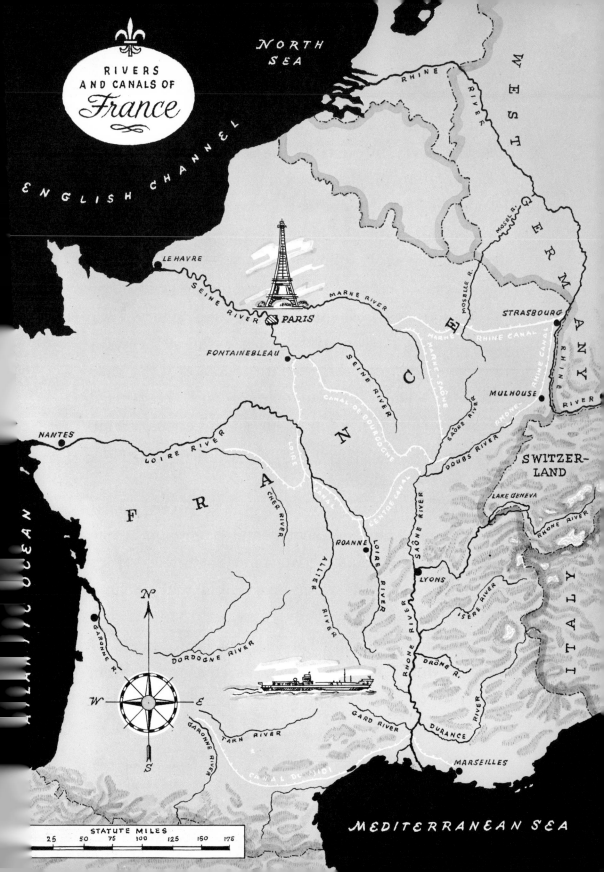

RIVERS
AND CANALS OF
France

NORTH
SEA

ENGLISH CHANNEL

LE HAVRE

PARIS

SEINE RIVER

FONTAINEBLEAU

MARNE RIVER

SEINE RIVER

CANAL DE BOURGOGNE

F R A N C E

NANTES

LOIRE RIVER

CHER RIVER

LOIRE CANAL

CENTRE CANAL

ROANNE

LOIRE RIVER

ALLIER RIVER

DORDOGNE RIVER

GARONNE R.

TARN RIVER

GARONNE RIVER

CANAL DU MIDI

GARD RIVER

RHINE
RIVER

WEST GERMANY

MOSEL R.

MOSELLE R.

STRASBOURG

MARNE-
RHINE CANAL

MARNE-SAÔNE

SAÔNE RIVER

RHÔNE-
RHINE CANAL

MULHOUSE

RHINE
RIVER

DOUBS RIVER

SWITZER-
LAND

LAKE GENEVA

RHONE RIVER

SAÔNE RIVER

LYONS

ISÈRE RIVER

DRÔME R.

RHÔNE RIVER

DURANCE

MARSEILLES

I T A L Y

ATLANTIC OCEAN

N
W   E
S

STATUTE MILES
25   50   75   100   125   150   175

MEDITERRANEAN SEA

In its earliest days, this river junction was a market place for one of the Gallic tribes. In 43 B.C., a group of Romans came up the Rhone and established a colony where Lyons now stands. The Roman name for the city was Lugdunum.

The fame of Lugdunum soon spread throughout the Roman Empire. The Emperor Augustus chose it as the seat of government, and every year representatives from sixty cities gathered here for the meeting of the Senate. As the Romans extended their European empire, they constructed magnificent roads reaching in all directions. From Lugdunum, these roads fanned out toward Spain, France, Switzerland and Italy.

In those days Lugdunum was a lively place. The Romans built a theater and a circular arena for spectacles and contests. Sometimes they flooded a place for water sports and make-believe sea battles.

Today on the riverbank there are traces of canals which, it is believed, carried water from the river to that ancient arena. In 1933 an almost

In 1933 this ancient Roman theater was discovered in Lyons.

perfectly preserved Roman theater was discovered. For years the people of Lyons had walked by the spot without knowing that an old Roman theater was under their feet. Now they have taken it for their own use and present outdoor plays there in the summer.

47

The city of Lyons in about 1879.

Lyons straddles the two rivers and the point of land between. To go from one part of the city to another you almost always have to cross some water. So Lyons is a city of bridges—twenty-seven in all. But there was a time when there was not even one.

In the Middle Ages people had neither the materials nor the knowledge that bridge builders have today. But Lyons was an important crossing

48

point. In the twelfth century a group of men called the Pontiff Brothers set out to put a bridge across the turbulent Rhone at Lyons. They were scholarly, religious men who were also skillful builders. They erected the bridge in sections. The first sections were of wood, which were then replaced by stone. After ten long years the bridge was finished. Soon an army of Crusaders came through on their long march to the Holy Land. It was King Richard the Lion-Hearted and his knights. As they clattered onto the new bridge, it collapsed under their massed weight.

Today little is left of the old bridges of Lyons. Twenty-three of the city's bridges were blown up during World War II. But the French rebuilt them quickly. Now you can stroll along the banks of the Saône and the Rhone, crossing back and forth at will.

During the sixteenth and seventeenth centuries, Lyons was an active business center. Its trade fairs were even more famous than those at Geneva. These fairs had been established by the

King of France in 1462. Special weeks were set aside for them four times a year.

At about this time Lyons became famous also for its beautiful silks. This rare material had first been made in the Far East—in China, Japan and India. It was brought to Europe by camel caravan over the desert and by ship across the water, along with spices and other goods from the East. Following the same trade routes from East to West came the knowledge of how to make this precious fabric.

Real silk is made from the cocoons of silkworms. These delicate creatures have to be carefully tended and fed, usually on mulberry leaves. When their cocoons are finished, the fragile strands are gently unwound and woven into silk cloth.

When it was found that silkworms could be cultivated in southern Europe, the Italians began to make their own silk. In the twelfth and thirteenth centuries, Italy was the center of silk weaving in Europe. Then the French kings be-

French Embassy Press and Information Division

An old silk loom of Lyons is shown at the left; a modern one at right.

came interested in this new craft and encouraged it. In 1450 Charles VII granted Lyons a monopoly for weaving silk. No other French city was permitted to compete. Later, King Francis I brought silkworms from Milan to be raised in the Rhone Valley.

A man came from Italy to set up the first mill. Weavers came from Genoa and Florence to operate the looms alongside the French workers.

Soon the mills were turning out beautiful silks for which Lyons became famous all over Europe.

In the seventeenth century 12,000 looms were said to be at work in the city. If you had been a French lady or gentleman of that time, the silk for your clothes would most likely have come from Lyons.

Silkworms are no longer cultivated in the valley of the Rhone. But Lyons has remained an important producer of textiles. Her mills are busy today turning out cloth of wool, cotton, silk and artificial fibers.

By the early 1500's, Lyons was buzzing with excitement of a new sort. It was not silk and silk mills. People took these for granted.

The great new invention was the printed book. Thanks to an ingenious German named Gutenberg, books could be printed in quantity. Before this each book was hand lettered and hand colored. Only a few books could be made, and these were written in Latin for churchmen and scholars.

After Gutenberg's invention, books became available to all who wanted to read and learn. They were printed in the language of the people

This early printing press was similar to an old cider or cheese press. It was the first to use movable metallic type that could be used again and again.

as well as in Latin. Never before did so many people turn to books.

In this great revolution of the spreading of knowledge, Lyons played an important part in France. The first book printed in the French language came off the presses of Lyons. The first book to be illustrated by wood-block prints was also made in Lyons.

Many well-known writers lived in Lyons in the sixteenth and seventeenth centuries. The famous playwright Molière and his troupe made Lyons their headquarters for several years in the seventeenth century.

Today most people think of Lyons as an industrial center. Instead of the Roman roads of the Emperor Agrippa, there are railroads and modern highways. The factories are busy turning out products useful for present-day life. But there are also many reminders of the past in Lyons. On one hill are the tall houses built by the early silk weavers. In narrow streets near the river there are houses which are even older, some of them built in the Middle Ages. And from a high hillside the Roman theater looks down on the city.

From the rooftop of the Cathedral of Notre-Dame de la Fourvière, this figure looks over the Saône and the Rhone rivers in Lyons.

This drawing of an ancient bas-relief in the Museum of Avignon shows men towing a boat up the Rhone. Casks held wine or oil.

6. Boats on the River

South of Lyons it is possible for boats to travel on the Rhone. But this river has never been a smooth or easy waterway. The current is strong, and often the passage is rough. Before the invention of the steam engine, boats floated downstream and had to be pulled back up. It took only three days to go from Lyons down to Arles. Sometimes it took as much as 30 days in the opposite direction.

One of the oldest river pictures we have shows two men pulling a tiny boat loaded with oil or wine casks. It is a little sculptured bas-relief made more than 1,900 years ago, before the birth of Christ. There is also a painting in the museum

Hauling on the Rhone.

at Lyons which shows teams of horses straining to pull a convoy of barges against the powerful current.

In the seventeenth and eighteenth centuries, travel by land was so uncomfortable that many travelers preferred riverboats south of Lyons. But the trip on the river seems to have been a frightening experience. Many well-known writers whose letters have been saved wrote about the terrors of the journey. At one time river bridges consisted of several stone arches supported by pillars in the

56

river bottom. The space between pillars was just wide enough for a boat to pass through. With a swift current, a boat might easily be hurled against a pillar. A boatman had to keep a sharp eye out all the time and steer carefully.

The river was especially treacherous at a place called La Voulte, "the turn," where the Drôme River comes in. Here two little islands get their names from the boatmen's warnings. One is called Printegarde, which means "watch out," and the other is Tenteben, meaning "hold tight."

In the eighteenth century the first steamboat

Lyons from Le Pont de Pierre, 1819.

built in France was tried out on the Saône River at Lyons. There are many paintings and drawings of this exciting event. While people watched from the banks, the great paddle wheels turned at the sides of the boat. They were more than a match for the strength of the current and pushed the boat upstream. It was the beginning of a new era in river travel. For many years after this, the Rhone was a busy highway. Ships moved majestically up and down carrying passengers and freight.

With the coming of the railroad, trucks and cars, the river lost much of its traffic. But barges and swift diesel-powered freight boats still transport goods on the Rhone. And in summer there is a pleasure boat for people who wish to enjoy a leisurely trip on the river highway.

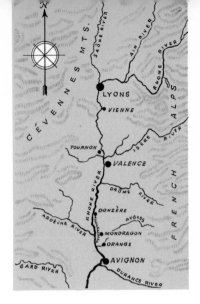

7. Ancient Ruins and Smoking Factories

As we follow the Rhone south from Lyons, we seem to move back and forth through time. Near the city the Rhone is shrouded by smoke from all the modern factories. But the air clears as we move away from the city. We pass a power plant just below Lyons. Then at Givors the river widens. Here is a calm stretch of water where jousting contests were held long ago. This is a sport in which men in boats competed with each other. Armed with long poles they tried to see which one could push the other out of the boat into the water. It was just a game for fun on holidays.

59

About 20 miles from Lyons we come to the city of Vienne. It nestles on a curve of the Rhone where the river Gère comes in. Rising high above the Rhone are the walls of an old Roman city. Against the hillside is an outdoor theater also built by the Romans.

In a busy square in the center of the town stands the perfect little Roman "Temple of Augustus and Livia." It was named for a Roman emperor and his wife. In many places the pagan Roman temples were destroyed when the people were converted to Christianity. This one was saved by being used as a church when the people of Vienne became Christian.

Besides Roman remains, there are many interesting ancient buildings in Vienne. The church of St. Pierre stands on the foundation of the oldest Christian church of the Gauls, built in the fourth century. On a terrace overlooking the Rhone rises the imposing church of Saint Maurice. This was constructed gradually in the course of several centuries, from the eleventh to the fifteenth.

60

Drawing of a sixteenth-century sculpture from Vienne, now in the Museum of Lyons.

Many people say it is the most impressive Gothic church between Lyons and the Mediterranean.

In the museums of Vienne are many fascinating things dug up in various parts of the city. One of the loveliest pieces of sculpture is the kneeling figure of a woman, known as the Venus of Vienne.

A fast modern highway runs along the Rhone at Vienne, linking Lyons with the south of France. Heavy trucks and fast cars speed along the edge of the little city not far from the ancient monuments. The residents of Vienne today go matter-of-factly about their daily lives, as people in any modern town. But wherever they go, they walk through streets full of reminders of all those who have lived before them, in this city on the Rhone.

After Vienne we come to Condrieu which is famous as the home of the best rivermen on the Rhone. These skilled boatmen were known as the Condrillots.

At Andance, still farther downriver, our eye is caught by three stark crosses silhouetted against the sky. It is said that during the Middle Ages three young women used to stand on this cliff looking down the Rhone. They were watching and waiting for their lovers who had gone off to the Holy Land on a Crusade. Many years went by, and finally the three girls gave up hope of ever seeing their lovers again. They threw themselves down from this cliff to die in the Rhone. The crosses stand here in their memory.

At Tournon is the first suspension bridge ever built across the Rhone. For the first time no pillars were put in the middle of the water. The

French Embassy Press and Information Division

On the eastern bank the hillside is covered with terraced vineyards.

bridge was hung from cables attached to towers at each end.

On the eastern bank of the river we see terraced land covered with grapevines. These are the Hermitage Vineyards, famed for their excellent wines. For many miles south of Tournon there are vineyards along the river. The wines are called "côtes du Rhône," which means "hillsides of the Rhone."

The next big town on the Rhone is Valence.

They say the "Midi" begins here. "Midi" is a word the French use for "south." It really means "midday." It suggests the blazing sun straight overhead, as one finds it in the Mediterranean area.

Not far below Valence the river Drôme comes in from the east. It is a small stream, but its valley is a beautiful one. If we had time to follow it back, we would find the hillsides dotted with the ruins of ancient castles.

As the Rhone flows through its wide valley toward the sea, it is flanked on both sides by mountains. In the distance to the east are the high French Alps. On the west lie the lower Cévennes Mountains, part of a range of highlands called by the French the Massif Central. Though not so high as the Alps, the Cévennes have some wild and rugged parts, especially on their western slopes. Sometimes water rushes down the sides of these mountains, making the Rhone flood suddenly.

In all its length from Lyons to the sea, the Rhone is a powerful and magnificent river. It moves through the lovely French countryside with an air of grandeur. Some French people have even compared it to a god, calling it *Le Fleuve Dieu*, (the god or god-like river).

But the engineers are learning to bring the mighty river under control. All along the course of the Rhone, one sees canals, dams and other engineering projects, always marked *aménagement du Rhône*, meaning the "regulation" or "managing" of the Rhone. The French have plans for

A passenger boat goes through the lock on the canal near Donzère.

controlling the river all the way from Lyons to the sea. Sometimes they divert part of the river from its natural bed to a smoother channel at the side. When they dam the Rhone, they make locks so that the boats can be raised or lowered to travel past the dam.

The French have three reasons for wanting to manage the Rhone. With dams they can convert its power into electricity. They also want to store and distribute water for irrigation. This will improve agricultural production. And to make navigation easier, they need to regulate the speed of the current and the steepness of the riverbed.

More and more below Valence we see that the Rhone is "managed." There is a big power plant at Beauchastel and another at Logis Neuf. One of the most ambitious engineering projects in the entire length of the river begins just after the town of Viviers. Part of the Rhone is led through a long wide canal several miles away from its natural course. This canal, which provides a smooth passage for boats, goes from Donzère to

From Donzère south to Mondragon, river traffic follows the canal.

Compagnie National du Rhône—J. Cellard

Walls of the Donzère-Mondragon Canal seem to tower over the ships.

Mondragon. Toward the end of this stretch is a dam and a huge generating plant at Bollène.

But all along the Rhone there is the contrast of the new and the old. Just after the canal rejoins the Rhone, the river Aygues comes in from the east. It is not a big river, but on its banks just a few miles from the Rhone stands the old Roman city of Orange. It is best known for its magnificent Roman theater.

We enter Orange by the triumphal arch as the Romans did in their time. In the middle of the city, the massive wall of the theater stands 120 feet high. Inside the theater we see that this wall is the back of the stage. In a niche high up in the wall overlooking the stage, the statue of the Emperor Augustus faces the audience as it did when Romans attended plays here. This is the only Roman theater left with such a complete wall and with the original statue of the emperor standing as it did in Roman times.

A play is rehearsed in the ruins of the Roman theater in Orange.
French Cultural Services

Le Pont Saint Bénézet in Avignon, 1480.

8. The Bridge at Avignon

At Avignon the Rhone is both broad and swift. In the middle of the river stands a wooded island, L'Isle de Barthelasse. A modern bridge, straddling the island, spans the river here. There are traffic

70

lights at each end to regulate the stream of cars crossing from one side of the Rhone to the other at this important point.

A few hundred yards upstream stands what is left of another, much older bridge, the Pont Saint Bénézet. This is the bridge described in the old French folk song:

Sur le pont d'Avignon
L'on y danse, l'on y danse
Sur le pont d'Avignon
L'on y danse tout en rond.

On the bridge of Avignon
There they dance, there they dance
On the bridge of Avignon
Each one dances in his turn.

This first bridge of Avignon was partly destroyed centuries ago by the turbulent waters of the Rhone. The three remaining arches reach out gracefully into the river, cut off in midstream. Only four of its original piles are still standing in the Rhone. On one is a tiny Romanesque chapel, dedicated to Saint Nicholas. But the bridge is named Pont Saint Bénézet in honor of its builder.

The Pont Saint Bénézet is very old. Its story goes back to the twelfth century. There was no bridge at Avignon then. But this was an important crossing point, and people wished to have a safe way of getting across the river. An attempt was made to erect a bridge, but the builders were finding it very difficult. A poor shepherd boy named Bénézet lived nearby. He came to the river and said that God had sent him to help build the bridge. Everyone laughed at the little boy. Partly as a joke he was told to lift one of the stones, much too heavy even for the strongest man. He picked it up easily and carried it to a position in the river. The laughing stopped. After this proof of his powers, the people believed that he had really been chosen by God to help construct the bridge. In the course of time he was called Saint Bénézet, and the bridge was named for him.

It took eleven years to build the bridge. Some descriptions say that it was more than three thousand feet long. Today not much is left of the

Only three arches are left of the Pont Saint Bénézet of Avignon.

old structure. But it is possible to walk on its remaining stone work to the little chapel. We know that as far back as the twelfth century the people of Avignon were walking and riding across the Rhone on Pont Saint Bénézet and—if the folk song is true—dancing on it. If they stopped to look down at the water, they saw the same Rhone we see today, flowing under its arches on its way to the sea.

Old as the bridge at Avignon is, the city is much older. Romans lived here in the first few centuries after the birth of Christ. Their name for the city was Avenio. Even before the Romans

73

The fourteenth century Palace of the Popes overlooks the Rhone.

came, this place on the Rhone was inhabited by a Gallic tribe called Cavares.

The most important event in Avignon's history, however, occurred in the fourteenth century.

For many years the headquarters of the Catholic church had been in Rome. But in 1309 a Frenchman was crowned Pope Clement V. He chose Avignon for his residence. For almost 70 years after this, the popes made Avignon their home. They built a magnificent palace on high ground at one end of the town. It was a fortress, too, to protect them from attack.

Scholars and diplomats and churchmen came to Avignon from all over Europe, and it became a very cosmopolitan city. It attracted so many poets and writers that it became known as a literary center. Petrarch, a famous Italian poet, lived at Avignon for many years. It was here that he saw a beautiful woman, Laura, whom he loved for the rest of his life. He wrote much of his poetry for her.

Eventually the popes moved back to Rome. But the imposing Palace of the Popes still stands in its dominating position overlooking the Rhone. From the steps in front of the palace, you can look down on the roofs and narrow, winding streets of the old medieval town.

The Castle of Tarascon looks as it did when built in the 1400's.

9. A Castle and a Monster

A few miles downstream from Avignon, the towns of Tarascon and Beaucaire face each other across the Rhone. Both were well known in the Middle Ages. There were fairs at Beaucaire which drew many visitors. It was also the setting of one of the most famous medieval stories of romance, about two lovers, Aucassin and Nicolette. Beaucaire had a castle built on a hill above the town.

But the most perfect castle to be found on the Rhone rises from the water's edge on the other side of the river at Tarascon. It belonged to King René, who lived in the fifteenth century. King

René loved pleasure and beautiful things. This magnificent castle shows his taste.

The parts which time had damaged have been completely restored. The Castle of Tarascon now looks exactly as it did when King René lived in it. You can cross the moat on a narrow bridge and enter through the old gate. You can wander through the enormous rooms, with their carved wooden ceilings and great fireplaces taller than a man. The curved stone staircase leads from one floor to the next until you come out on the parapet at the top. Looking down inside the walls, you see the formal garden laid out as it used to be, with flower beds in elaborate patterns. It is easy to imagine King René and his courtiers and ladies walking along the flower-bordered paths in the cool of the evening. But if you happen to glance in the other direction, at the Rhone, you may be brought quickly back to the twentieth century. For there you may see a modern freight boat passing close by the castle walls.

One of the legends of Tarascon tells of a monster, the Tarasque. This was a dreadful creature, part dragon and part lion, which devoured everything that came its way. People said that this part of the Rhone was the haunt of the Tarasque. Everyone was terrified by this beast. But finally it was subdued by a gentle saint named Martha. A church built at Tarascon in the twelfth century was dedicated to her and called the Church of Saint Martha. But the town still bears the name Tarascon, from the monster, the Tarasque.

F R A N C E
THE
RHONE
DELTA
CANAL
RIVER
AVIGNON
RHONE
DURANCE
BEAUCAIRE
TARASCON
DURANCE RIVER
CANAL
CANAL
RHONE
ARLES
AIGUESMORTES
LITTLE
BIG RHONE
CANAL
PORT ST. LOUIS DU RHONE
ÉTANG DE BERRE
CANAL
MARTIGUES
CANAL
LES SAINTES-MARIES-DE-LA-MER
MARSEILLES
W
E
MEDITERRANEAN SEA

10. Through the Delta to the Sea

The last big city on the Rhone is Arles. Here the river divides into two branches, the Big Rhone and the Little Rhone. The Big Rhone continues south, while the Little Rhone veers somewhat to the west. The river now travels 230 miles from Lyons to the Mediterranean. It was not always so far. At one time a bay of the sea extended all the way up to Arles, and the Rhone ended there.

Arles has played many different parts in the history of this section of France. The size of its Roman arena tells how big and active it was under its Roman name, Arelate. Twenty-five thousand people could be seated in the enormous amphitheater, to watch the combats and spectacles which the Romans loved. It was the Romans who gave this part of France the name it has today. They called it *provincia nostra* meaning "our province." We have changed it only a little and call it Provence.

When Christianity came to France, Arles became the seat of a bishopric. In the middle of the city stands a reminder of this period in Arles' history, the graceful and charming Cloister of St. Trophime. It is dedicated to a Greek disciple, Trophime, who taught Christianity to the people of Provence.

In the nineteenth century musicians, painters and writers were inspired by the Mediterranean warmth of Provence. Many of the sun-drenched canvases of Vincent van Gogh were painted near

Arles. Georges Bizet, the composer of the opera "Carmen," also wrote an orchestral suite called "L'Arlésienne."

The French say you can believe only half of what you hear in Provence. They claim that people with the Provençal temperament like to dramatize and exaggerate. Certainly Provence has a character all its own. It is Mediterranean as well as French. There is the brilliance of the sun and a liveliness and warmth not to be found farther north.

Between the two arms of the Rhone south of Arles lies the delta, called by the French *the Camargue.* It is a marshy, salty plain built up in the course of centuries by the gravel and silt

The small black cattle of the Camargue cross the marshy meadows.
French Government Tourist Office

Cowboys, called "gardians," live in the great plain region of Camargue.

which the Rhone has brought in its journey from the mountains to the sea.

You will find cowboys in the Camargue, riding beautiful white horses and tending herds of small black bulls. But they are not called *cowboys* in French. In the Camargue they are known as *gardians*.

In this marshy country there are salt pans,

where the sea water is held back to evaporate. Here you will see little hills of salt, collected from the pans, waiting to be shipped away.

Recently the Camargue has also become the rice basket of France. In the flat, easily flooded fields the delicate green plants grow well in the shallow water.

On the delta of the Rhone are two towns with strange names. One is called Aiguesmortes, meaning "dead waters." The other is Les Saintes-Maries-de-la-Mer. This is French for "The Saint Marys of the Sea." Like so many towns along the Rhone, their names come from events far back in time.

Today Les Saintes-Maries-de-la-Mer is a seaside resort. In summer its beach is overrun by visitors. They come to bask in the sun and swim in the warm waters of the Mediterranean. In the town not far from the crowded beach stands a stark, simple church. It rises out of the town like a ship on the sea. On a wall near the entrance is a carved wooden picture showing three women in

Drawing of a bas-relief in wood at the church of the Saint Marys.

a small boat. They are Mary Jacobé, the sister
of the Virgin Mary; Mary Salomé, the mother
of the disciple James; and their servant, Sarah.

The legend of Les Saintes Maries says that
seven years after the death of Christ these three
were driven out of the Holy Land. Most versions
of the story say there was a third Mary with
them—Mary Magdalene. They all set off in a
small boat, without oars or sails. But angels were

guiding the helpless women. They made the dangerous crossing of the sea and landed at this spot on the northern shore of the Mediterranean. And they stayed where the angels had brought them safely to shore. Later the church was built here in their memory. Both the town and the church have been known ever since as The Saint-Marys-of-the-Sea.

The rest of the story is that Sarah, the servant, was chosen by the gypsies as their patron saint.

Pilgrims reach out to touch the caskets of two of the Saint Marys.
French Government Tourist Office

A gypsy holds his child to kiss the cheek of the statue of Saint Sarah.

Each year there is a gathering of these wandering people in the Camargue. They come in trucks and wagons, their traveling homes, carrying all their possessions with them. Pots and pans hang from the sides. They camp for the night wherever they stop. In their colorful clothes—long skirts and bright sashes and jingling bracelets—they walk in procession through the streets. The men carry the dark figure of the servant Sarah through the town on their shoulders. Their part of the church is the dark lower crypt. Here they go to

The walls of Aiguesmortes stand as they did in the 13th century.

honor their own patron saint and give thanks for that safe voyage made so many hundreds of years ago.

Aiguesmortes, too, has its links with the past. Its grim fortifications are a reminder of ancient battles and lost campaigns. It stands on a dry plain, with a man-made canal by it leading to the sea. Its surroundings are proof of the changing course of history and of the Rhone itself. Its name tells part of its story.

Aiguesmortes once heard the sound of water lapping at the shore. It stood near the Mediterranean and on one bank of the Rhone. But rivers which wash away earth in one place

88

make new land in another. Just as the Mississippi has enlarged its delta, the Rhone moved the shore line at Aiguesmortes. The slow deposit of mud and silt carried by the river made land where water used to be. Long after this had happened the Rhone itself deserted Aiguesmortes. Once, because of a flood or a weakened bank, the Rhone broke away from its old bed and made a new channel. The Little Rhone no longer flows by the town. It follows a course more than six miles to the east, near Les Saintes-Maries-de-la-Mer.

Aiguesmortes is well named "dead waters" now. But in the thirteenth century it was a busy port of embarkation for the Crusades. In August, 1248, King Louis IX sailed from Aiguesmortes with his knights on a Crusade to free the Holy Land. They had spent four years preparing for the voyage, and King Louis was hopeful of success. But he was taken prisoner in Egypt, then ransomed and returned to France. King Louis was a brave and determined man. Though ill, he organized another expedition and set sail again from Aiguesmortes in 1270. A few weeks later he died of plague in Tunis.

Though he did not achieve success in the Crusades, Louis IX was loved and respected as a good king. The people called him a saint.

Centuries have passed since Saint Louis sailed away from Aiguesmortes, but he is still remembered. His statue stands in the square inside the walled town, and the cathedral is dedicated to him. A harbor on the Big Rhone some distance away is named Port Saint Louis. There have been changes in the course of the Rhone and the shore of the Mediterranean. But the towers and walls of Aiguesmortes stand exactly as they did in the thirteenth century.

The Rhone nears its end in a landscape of marshes and bays. The branches of the river have followed different channels at different times. Artificial canals have also been cut to open passages to the sea. Because the Rhone has not just one mouth but several, this section is called *Les Bouches du Rhône*—the mouths of the Rhone.

Houses of the gardians are on the marshy plain of the Camargue.

The end of the Rhone has never provided a good harbor on the Mediterranean. Sandbanks often block the passage for boats. Marseilles has an excellent harbor, but it is not exactly at the end of the Rhone. So the French have gone to great trouble to connect the Rhone with Marseilles.

Near the end of the major branch of the Rhone is a big pond, the Étang de Berre. This used to be a quiet backwater where you would find fish and birds, and sometimes artists painting the peaceful scene. It has become a busy commercial area, lined with oil refineries and factories. Canals

By this four-mile tunnel, ships from the Rhone come to Marseilles.

have been made, leading to this pond from Arles
and from the Big Rhone. Then through the neck
of land separating the pond and Marseilles, a
tunnel, four miles long, has been cut. This dark
waterway, called the Tunnel du Rove, permits
barges coming down the Rhone to reach Marseilles
and the Mediterranean Sea.

92

Through many varied channels in the delta, the Rhone at last reaches the Mediterranean. Where its waters merge with the sea, the sea turns a bit cooler. For the Rhone carries with it to its end a hint of its Alpine beginnings. It reminds us that it was a river of Switzerland before it became a river of France.

At its end, as all along its course, the Rhone is a river of contrasts. The tankers and oil refineries belong to the Rhone. And so do the ancient walls of Aiguesmortes. The Rhone is as modern as the dams and power plants, and older than the legend of the three Marys. It is as timeless as the mountain mists where it begins, and the watery marshes where it flows into the sea. All are part of the story of the Rhone.

Index

Aiguesmortes, 84, 88–90
Alps, 9–20, 21–27
Andance, 62
Andermatt, 9
Animal and plant life, 18–19, 26–27, 39
Arles, 55, 80–81
Arve River, 38
Augustus, Roman Emperor, 46, 69
Avignon, 2, 70–75
Aygues River, 68

Beaucaire, 77
Bénézet, 72
Bernese Oberland, 21
Boats and boating, 33, 39, 42, 43, 55–58, 59, 62, 66, 78, 91
Book printing and reading, 52–53
Bridges, 2, 17, 22, 24, 48–49, 56, 62, 70–73, 78
Brig, 24–26

Camargue, see Delta
Canals, 43–45, 66–68, 88, 90, 91–92
Castles, 27, 28, 42, 76–78
Cévennes Mountains, 64
Christianity, 28, 30, 60, 81
Clement V, Pope, 74
Cowboys, see Gardians
Crusades, 49, 62, 89–90

Dams, see Locks and dams
Delta (Camargue), 82–93
Dents du Midi, 30
Donzère-Mondragon Canal, 65, 66–68

Drance River, 30
Drôme River, 64

Edelweiss, 19
Étang de Berre, 91–92

Factories, 52, 59, 91
Fishing, 39, 42
Floods, 24, 64
Flowers, Alpine, 18–19
Furka Pass, 9, 14, 15, 16

Gardians (cowboys), 83, 91
Geneva, 34–37, 38
Genissiat Dam, 40–41
Gère River, 60
Glacial clay, 24
Glacial water, 38
Glaciers, 10, 11, 12–17
Grimsel Pass, 9
Gutenberg, Johannes, 52–53
Gypsies, 86–88

Icebergs, 12
Ile Rousseau, 37
Isle de Barthelasse, 70–71
Italy, 21, 34, 36

Lake Geneva, 30–32, 33–37
Legends, 62, 72, 78–79, 85–86
Locks and dams, 36, 38–39, 40–41, 65–68
Loire River, 44
Louis IX, King of France, 89–90
Lugdunum, see Lyons
Lyons, 42, 43–44, 46–54, 55–56, 57, 58, 61

Maps, 8, 21, 33, 45, 59, 80
Marseilles, 44, 91
Martigny, 30
Matterhorn, 27
Mauritius, 30–31
Maximian, Roman Emperor, 30–31
Mediterranean Sea, 20, 44, 80, 84,
    88, 91–93
Monster of Tarascon, 78–79
Mont Blanc, 30, 38

Name of river, 7
Napoleon I, 25, 29
North Sea, 44

Orange, 68

Palace of the Popes, Avignon, 74–
    75
Paris, 44
Petrarch, 75
Pont de Pierre, 58
Pont Saint Bénézet, 2, 70, 71–73
Pontiff Brothers, 49
Port Saint Louis, 90
Power plants, 38, 40–41, 59, 66–68
Printing industry, 52–53
Protestant Reformation, 36
Provence, 81–82

Railroads, 25–26, 54
René I, 77–78
Rhine River, 20, 44
Rhodanic Republic, 29
Rhone Glacier, 9, 10, 11, 13, 14–17,
    32
Richard the Lion-Hearted, 49
Roads, 9, 11, 14–15, 24–25, 27, 30,
    31, 46, 54, 61
Romans, 7, 27–28, 30–31, 46, 54, 60,
    68–69, 73, 81

Rousseau, Jean Jacques, 37

Saint Bénézet, 72
Saint Bernard dogs, 14
Saint Bernard Pass, 14, 30
Saint Martha, 79
Saint-Maurice, 30–31
Saint Sarah, 87
Saint Trophime, 81
Saintes-Maries-de-la-Mer, Les, 84–
    88, 89
Salt pans, 83–84
Saône River, 43–44, 49, 57
Seine River, 44
Silk industry, 50–52
Simplon Pass and Tunnel, 25–26
Sion, 27–29, 31, 32
Source of river, 16–17
Switzerland, 9–37, 44, 93

Tarascon, 76–79
Textile industry, 44, 50–52
Theaters, Roman, 46–47, 54, 68–69
Tournon, 62–63
Tower of the Witches, Sion, 32
Trade fairs, 34–35, 49–50, 77
Transportation, 24–26, 32, 42, 43–
    44, 46, 54, 55–58, 61
Tunnels, 11, 25–26, 92

Valais, 21–32
Valence, 63–64, 66
Van Gogh, Vincent, 81–82
Vertrieu, 41–42
Vienne, 60–62
Villages, Alpine, 18–19, 22–23
Vineyards, 26, 27, 63
Visp River, 27

Zermatt, 26, 27

FRANCES WILLARD VON MALTITZ was born in Maine and graduated from Wheaton College in Norton, Massachusetts. She received her master's degree from Teachers College, Columbia University. She has taught at Wheaton and at Greensboro College in North Carolina.

With her husband, a New York lawyer, she has traveled widely throughout Europe and Latin America. Her first book, *The Rhone: River of Contrasts*, grew out of one of these trips.

Fluent in both French and German, Mrs. von Maltitz is a free-lance reader and translator in these languages for various American publishers.

In addition, she serves as a School Volunteer in New York City, teaching children in crowded mid-city schools. Her *Saturday Review* article about this experience, "Portrait of P.S. 2," won wide acclaim.

When not traveling, Mr. and Mrs. von Maltitz spend the winters in their Greenwich Village apartment and their summers near Weston, Connecticut.